JURASSIC
TOWEL ORIGAMI

JURASSIC
TOWEL ORIGAMI

The craft that bath time forgot!
Alison Jenkins

Andrews McMeel
Publishing

Kansas City

ANDREWS McMEEL PUBLISHING, LLC,
An Andrews McMeel Universal company,
1130 Walnut Street,
Kansas City, Missouri 64106.

ISBN-13: 978-0-7407-7856-8
ISBN-10: 0-7407-7856-0

This book was conceived,
designed, and produced by

Ivy Press
The Old Candlemakers, West Street,
Lewes, East Sussex, BN7 2NZ, UK.

Creative Director Peter Bridgewater
Publisher Jason Hook
Editorial Director Caroline Earle
Senior Editor Lorraine Turner
Publishing Assistant Katie Ellis
Art Director Clare Harris
Concept Design Wayne Blades
Design JC Lanaway
Photographer Andrew Perris
Photoshop Artwork Clare Harris,
Kate Haynes, and Wayne Blades

Printed in Thailand.

09 10 CTP 11 12 10 9 8 7 6 5 4 3 2 1

CONTENTS

INTRODUCTION

The recent discovery of a shower stall-shaped cave deep in the heart of the Japanese mountains, littered with extraordinary little fossils, caused excited speculation as much as confused scratching of heads among the paleontology community. The fossils appeared to be made of plant fiber, which had been folded into exquisite reptilian replicas of many species of dinosaur. Years of careful laboratory research have finally produced an earth-shattering conclusion: these were in fact the earliest examples of folded towels. Yes, towel origami is prehistoric!

Jurassic Towel Origami offers you the Neanderthal—yet strangely contemporary—opportunity to indulge in a spot of pre-civilization towel folding before bath time. Amaze your houseguests and celebrate your ancestors by creating any one of 15 distinctive towel models, from a Brachiosaurus to Stonehenge. While every effort has been taken to ensure the reader has as much fun as possible, the same does not apply to chronological accuracy! Inspiration has been plucked indiscriminately from various points in prehistory, so you can sit your caveman next to T. rex, and Pteranodon can soar over Stonehenge without fear!

Wondering where to start? All you need to do is equip yourself with a pile of fluffy bath towels and let your imagination travel back in time a few million years … then take a peek at the section on Basic Body and Head Shapes *(see pages 10–14)*.

The projects

Each origami model is simply but carefully described, using just eight steps, and is illustrated from the very first fold to the final finishing touch. You will notice that each project has a skill rating: easy, moderate, or difficult *(see right)*. If you are new to this ancient art, you are advised to begin with an easy—but equally effective—model, such as the Plesiosaur *(see page 28)*, and then progress to something more elaborate that involves a little careful manipulation, such as T. rex *(see page 72)*; or indeed you could go for a winged model like the Pteranodon *(see page 40)* or the Dimorphodon *(see page 64)*, which requires the use of a shower rail for suspension purposes!

The embellishments suggested for each project can be found among your household items: buttons, rubber gloves, saucepan scouring pads, clothespins, elastic hairbands, and so on. However, you can use anything that takes your fancy in your attempt to re-create a prehistoric scene in your bathroom. Indeed, if the creative juices really begin to flow, you can invent your own unique dinosaur, by combining different head and body shapes with assorted horns and fins. After all, archaeologists guess a little when they put fossilized bones together.

So don't waste one prehistoric minute: discover your inner cave person with *Jurassic Towel Origami*—the craft that bath time forgot!

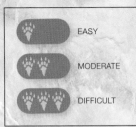

SKILL RATINGS

🐾	EASY
🐾	MODERATE
🐾	DIFFICULT

🦕 Brachiosaurus: easy

🦕 Dimetrodon: easy

🦕 Elasmosaurus: easy

🦕 Plesiosaur: easy

🦕 Stonehenge: easy

🦕 Euplocephalus: moderate

🦕 Pteranodon: moderate

🦕 Stegosaurus: moderate

🦕 Triceratops: moderate

🦕 Velociraptor: moderate

🦕 Woolly mammoth: moderate

🦕 Caveman: difficult

🦕 Dimorphodon: difficult

🦕 Saber-toothed tiger: difficult

🦕 Tyrannosaurus rex: difficult

TOWEL BASICS AND TIPS

The first step in making a towel origami model is to lay out a towel flat on your work surface—the floor, the bed, or wherever you feel most comfortable. This towel is laid out either horizontally or vertically and is then folded or rolled (or a combination of both techniques) to achieve the desired size and shape. Each set of instructions indicates in the first step which way you need to orient the towel.

Basic materials

Essentially you need a pile of your fluffiest towels (see below for recommended sizes), plus a little time and patience. We have suggested suitably colored towels for the dinosaur models, but you can really let your imagination run wild and go for something completely different, if the mood strikes you; archaeologists have little idea what color dinosaurs were, so you can make them any shade or pattern you like. Some of the models need a helping hand to stay upright, so you may need to make use of a few supports in the form of toilet rolls, shampoo bottles, and so on.

TOWEL SIZES

Towels can vary quite a lot in size, but the ones used for our models conform roughly to the dimensions given below. Don't worry if your own towels are slightly smaller or larger—it won't matter too much.

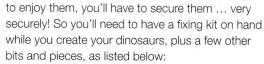 Face cloth: 13 x 13 in/33 x 33 cm

Hand towel: 20 x 40 in/50 x 100 cm

Bath towel: 27 x 51 in/68 x 130 cm

Fixing kit

In order to make sure that your models don't collapse before your guests have had a chance to enjoy them, you'll have to secure them … very securely! So you'll need to have a fixing kit on hand while you create your dinosaurs, plus a few other bits and pieces, as listed below:

• Safety pins, for securing overlaps and body parts
• Double-sided adhesive tape, for positioning eyes and other features
• Clothespins, for holding thick layers in place and for support
• Dressmaker's glass-headed pins, for securing sponge shapes
• Sharp scissors, tracing paper, and pencil, for making templates (see pages 76–79) and for cutting out shapes

Basic folds

Many projects begin with a towel laid out horizontally, then folded in half widthways to make a square; or with a towel laid out vertically, then folded lengthways to make a long, narrow band. Where the model requires you to fold the towel into thirds or make a fold of a certain depth, first indicate the fold position in the pile with the tip of your finger; you can then use that line as a folding guide.

Basic rolls

The rolling technique can be performed in one of two ways: parallel or diagonal. Parallel rolls are made by rolling the towel in from both long or short ends to meet at the center, running in line with the edge. Diagonal rolls are made from one corner of the towel or folded shape, or along a diagonal fold made in a previous step, obliquely across the towel to the other side (or from both sides to meet at the center).

TOWEL LAID OUT HORIZONTALLY

Fold in half widthways.   Fold in half lengthways.

PARALLEL ROLL

Roll one edge toward the center.   Roll the other edge toward the center.

TOWEL LAID OUT VERTICALLY

Fold in half widthways.   Fold in half lengthways.

DIAGONAL ROLL

Roll from lower corner.

SAFETY NOTE

If you have used safety pins, do make sure that you remove them all before using the towels for bathing; an open safety pin can easily scratch the skin, and a closed one can snag the fluffy pile of your towels.

FOLDING INTO THIRDS

Divide into three horizontally.   Divide into three vertically.

CREASING

Make a visible crease.

BASIC BODY AND HEAD SHAPES

The following step-by-step instructions will guide you through a few basic towel origami shapes, and some tricky ones, too—in fact, all you need to know to start creating your own Jurassic menagerie! It's worth practicing the techniques a few times before starting your models.

Body shape 1

This useful body shape looks rather like a plucked chicken! It forms the basis for the Velociraptor *(see page 52)*, Dimetrodon *(see page 20)*, Stegosaurus *(see page 44)*, Euplocephalus *(see page 36)*, Elasmosaurus *(see page 24)*, and Dimorphodon *(see page 64)*.

1 Lay the towel out horizontally, then indicate the center by drawing your finger through the pile vertically down the middle of the towel. Roll both short sides toward the center point.

2 Grasp the rolled-up shape at both ends and flip it over to the other side. Then bend the shape in half so that all four rolled ends meet, as shown.

3 Holding the rolled shape with one hand, locate the corners of the towel that lie inside each of the rolled ends. Pull these corners out a little, and grasp them in both hands as shown.

4 Now stretch your arms wide to pull out the rolls and form a slim body shape with four "limbs." The shape can be pinned together at the center if necessary, then manipulated to suit the requirements of the model in question.

Body shape 2

This is a combination of two shapes: arched legs and a back and tail structure. One, both, or variations of these shapes have been used to create the Tyrannosaurus rex *(see page 72)*, Triceratops *(see page 48)*, Euplocephalus *(see page 36)*, and woolly mammoth *(see page 56)*.

TIP You can also use two towels together to make a thicker leg shape.

Body shape 2a

1 Lay the towel out horizontally. Make a fold of approximately 4 in/10 cm along both lower and upper edges. Now roll each of the short sides toward the center point.

2 Grasp the rolled shape at both ends and bend it over to form a soft curved arch. The rolls can be secured with safety pins, if necessary. You can also open out the folds at the base of each leg to increase its stability.

Body shape 2b

1 Lay the towel out horizontally, then fold it in half by bringing the left-hand short edge over to meet the right-hand edge *(see page 9)*.

2 Now fold the upper and lower left-hand corners, and the lower right-hand corner, toward the center point of the square shape created in step 1.

3 Pick up the folded edges at the bottom right and top left and roll them diagonally toward the center of the shape, to meet in the center, then safety pin them together. You can also fold the shape up loosely for a wider, flatter appearance and safety pin it, if you wish.

4 Now flip the shape over to the other side so that any pins and the overlap are on the underside. Place the finished back and tail structure onto the arched legs—Body shape 2a (or Body shape 1)—in order to continue the model's construction.

Body shape 3

This shape can be manipulated to sit in an upright position, which is useful for the Tyrannosaurus rex *(see page 72)*, saber-toothed tiger *(see page 68)*, and caveman *(see page 60)*.

1 You need an extra towel for this model to act as padding for the main body. Lay the extra towel out horizontally, then fold it into three widthways. Now roll the shape up loosely, beginning at the lower short edge, to form a soft cylindrical pad.

2 Lay the towel in the specified color out vertically, then place the rolled pad in the center, about 4 in/10 cm down from the upper short edge. Bring the left-hand long edge over the cylindrical pad.

3 Pick up the right-hand long edge and bring it toward the center, overlapping the left-hand side. Use a few large safety pins at this point to secure the overlap.

4 Now open out the lower short edge of the towel and roll it up toward the wrapped pad. You can secure the roll to the base of the pad at the center, if necessary.

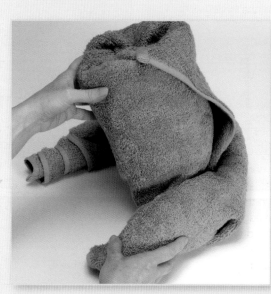

5 Slip your hand underneath the padded body shape and sit it upright, placing it on a container or toilet roll to give it extra height, if you wish. Tighten the roll made in step 4, tucking the loose top end of the towel into the padding. Arrange the ends to resemble "legs" around the base of the body, or as the model requires.

Head shape 1

This head shape has an upper and lower jaw—perfect for inserting a row or two of pearly white teeth. Use it for Tyrannosaurus rex *(see page 72)* and the saber-toothed tiger *(see page 68)*.

1 Lay the towel out horizontally, then make vertical indentations in the pile at the quarter and halfway points using your fingertip. Roll the left-hand short edge toward the quarter mark on the left side.

2 Place a finger halfway down the roll, then bring the top corner down to the center to form a right angle. Bring the bottom corner up to the center to make a pointed shape on the left-hand side, which will form the lower jaw.

3 Bring the upper and lower edges toward the center, covering the ends of the rolls and securing them with a safety pin.

4 Repeat the actions in steps 1 and 2 on the right-hand side, to form the upper jaw.

5 Fold the shape in half, bringing the lower jaw over to sit on top of the top jaw.

6 Slip your hand under the head shape and flip it over to the other side. Pull the edges of the top jaw around the lower jaw. Use a large safety pin to secure the overlap.

7 Manipulate the rolls and fold it to fit the requirements of your model. Use two colored elastic hairbands to form small rounded ears on the top of the head, if necessary.

TIP If, having mastered all the techniques described on these pages, you find yourself in a creative mood, you can combine different head and body shapes to design some dinosaurs of your own.

Head shape 2

This involves a tight diagonal roll to form a neat triangular shape; variations on the shape and size of the towel will result in a shorter or longer head. This design is used for the Triceratops (see page 48) and the woolly mammoth (see page 56).

1 Lay the towel out horizontally. Now fold it into three widthways (see page 9).

> **TIP** For a longer, more pointed shape, fold the towel in half at step 1.

2 Grasp the lower left-hand corner and roll it tightly in a diagonal fashion toward the center point. Do the same with the upper left-hand corner. You can secure the resulting pointed head with a few large safety pins, if you wish.

3 If the design requires it, flip the shape over to the other side so that the "face" is uninterrupted by folds. Pull out the corners that lie inside the rolls at the top to form ears, if necessary.

Head shape 3

This shape is used for the caveman (see page 60) because it is compact and rounded, with a large mouth that can be manipulated into a wide grin if necessary!

1 Lay the towel out horizontally. Then fold it in half by bringing the left-hand short edge over to meet the right-hand edge (see page 9).

2 Roll the upper edge of the resulting square shape in tightly to the center point, then repeat with the lower edge to make a parallel roll.

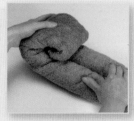

3 Now roll the shape into a tight ball, beginning at the left-hand corner.

4 Holding the rolled ball firmly in one hand, grasp the outer layer of the open end of the towel in the other hand and peel it right back over the rolled ball. This secures the head shape and forms the mouth. Secure the overlap with a safety pin.

THE PROJECTS

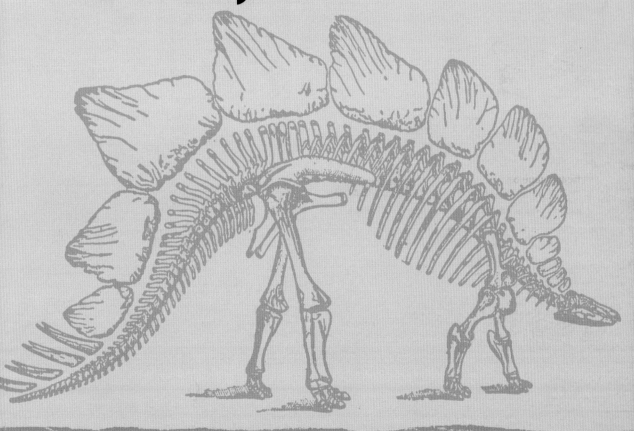

BRACHIOSAURUS

The Brachiosaurus was certainly a giant of the dinosaur world, both in height and bulk. His head could tower 39 ft/12 m above the ground, his length from nose to tail could stretch to 246 ft/75 m, and that's not to mention his weight—Brachiosaurus weighed in at about 69 tons/70 tonnes! Despite those impressive statistics, this dino was a gentle giant, an herbivore that spent his time nibbling tender leaves at the tops of the highest trees, much as giraffes do today.

YOU WILL NEED

- 3 beige bath towels
- 2 buttons/plastic eyes
- fixing kit *(see page 8)*

Make your own Brachiosaurus

1 Lay one bath towel out vertically. Fold both long sides in by about 6 in/15 cm, then press the folds flat using the palm of your hand. Roll the upper and lower short edges to meet at the center, securing them with two safety pins.

2 Grasp the rolled towel at each end and bend it to form an arch shape. Splay out the end of each roll a little so the arch stands steadily, forming the legs.

3 For the body and tail, lay the second bath towel out vertically. Crease a horizontal center line. Fold the top left-hand corner over to the center, then fold the top right-hand corner over to the center, to form an arrow. Press flat. Fold the bottom left-hand corner up to the center, then fold the bottom right-hand corner over to the center, to form a diamond. Press flat.

4 Roll the resulting top and lower points toward the center, then secure the rolls together with a safety pin.

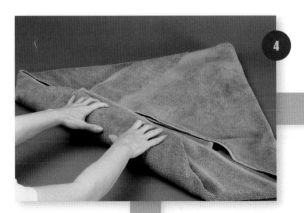

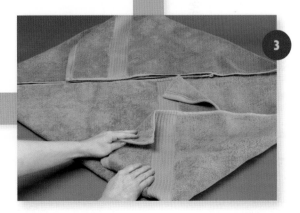

5 Slip your hand underneath the rolled body and flip it over to the other side. Lift the shape gently and place it on top of the arched legs, as shown. Fold the left-hand point down to form a flat chest area against which to rest the head and neck. You can now arrange the right-hand point to form the tail.

6 To make the head and neck, lay the remaining towel out vertically. Bring the top and bottom left-hand corners in to meet at the center, then fold in the right-hand corners, as shown.

7 Grasp the lower fold and roll it tightly toward the center. Do the same with the other fold to make a parallel roll. Secure the rolls together with three safety pins, then flip over to the other side.

8 Place the lower end of the head and neck roll against the dinosaur's chest. Use safety pins to secure it to the legs and body, then arrange the neck into a gentle arched shape. Secure two buttons or wibbly-wobbly eyes to the head with small tabs of double-sided adhesive tape.

TIP The Brachiosaurus is quite a top-heavy shape, so make sure the leg rolls are secure and steady before you attach the body and neck—otherwise he may collapse!

DIMETRODON

Dimetrodon's characteristic feature was the sail-like fin running along his back, probably used to keep the poor fellow cool in the heat of the day! These mammal-like reptiles existed on Earth between 280 and 260 million years ago, and though their limbs were fairly small, they were probably quite agile and pretty good at catching their dinner. When not in active pursuit of food, Dimetrodon loves to relax in modern-day bathrooms in all parts of the world.

YOU WILL NEED

- 3 blue bath towels
- 1 blue elastic hairband
- 1 striped dish cloth
- 2 buttons/plastic eyes
- 1 yellow kitchen sponge
- fixing kit *(see page 8)*

Make your own Dimetrodon

1 Lay one bath towel out horizontally. Roll both short ends inward to the center, then proceed to construct Body shape 1 *(see page 10)*. Secure the center folds with a large safety pin.

2 Lay the second bath towel out horizontally. Bring both long edges to meet in the center. Fold the left-hand corners toward the center to form a point. Then bring the upper and lower long folds to meet in the center, forming a long band.

3 Gather the roll up about 6 in/15 cm from the left-hand end, winding the blue hairband tightly around the shape to form the head. Tuck in and manipulate the folds at the pointed end, to add some character.

4 Place the roll onto the body, as shown, then tuck the right-hand end underneath the center of the body. This will form a soft pad and will act as a support, raising the body slightly. At this point you can arrange the four legs neatly.

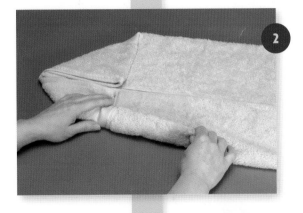

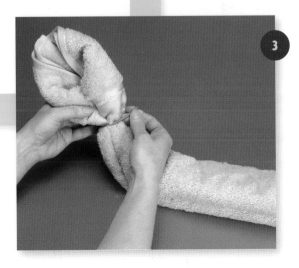

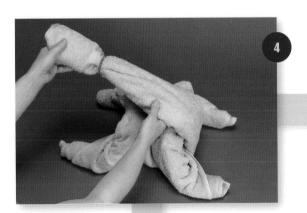

5 To make the back and tail, lay the remaining bath towel out vertically, then fold it in half by bringing the top-hand short edge over to meet the bottom-hand edge. Fold the upper left-hand corner toward the center, then roll the shape diagonally, beginning at the lower left-hand corner.

6 Place the back and tail roll onto the body shape, positioning the blunt end just behind the head. Use a large safety pin to secure the hairband around the neck to the back/tail roll; this will support the head and neck.

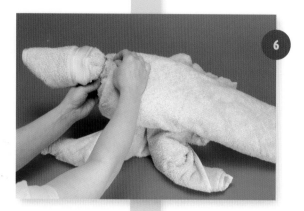

7 Trace onto paper and then cut out the fin template *(see page 77)*. Cut out two shapes from the striped dish cloth. Join the short straight edges together with double-sided adhesive tape to form a long band that is curved at each end. Pleat up the cloth, using your fingers to press the folds flat.

8 Fix the pleated fin along the spine of the Dimetrodon using clothespins. To complete the model, use tabs of double-sided adhesive tape to secure the buttons or eyes in place, then cut out a forked tongue (using the template on page 77) from the yellow sponge and place it the mouth.

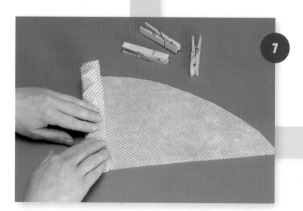

ELASMOSAURUS

Elasmosaurus is never happier than when up to his neck in water; and speaking of necks ... this dino holds the record for one of the longest. Skeletal evidence suggests that the neck was usually longer than the body and could contain up to 75 vertebrae, while the body and neck could stretch to a total of 46 ft/14 m in length! Elasmosaurus would paddle or swim along in the water, using his agile, snakelike neck to catch fish and other marine delicacies.

YOU WILL NEED

- 3 lime-green bath towels
- 1 extra bath towel for neck padding (any color, optional)
- 1 yellow kitchen sponge
- 2 buttons/plastic eyes
- fixing kit (see page 8)

Make your own Elasmosaurus

1 With one green bath towel, construct Body shape 1 *(see page 10)*. Use a few large safety pins to secure the folds at the center so that the shape remains formed while you make the rest of the model.

2 Lay the second green bath towel out horizontally. Fold the bottom left-hand corner inward, then roll up the towel in a diagonal fashion, beginning at the lower right-hand corner, to form the body and tail.

3 Lay the rolled-up shape onto the body shape formed in step 1. At this point you can arrange the folds that run along the sides of the body above the legs into a pleasing line.

4 Take the remaining green bath towel and lay it out horizontally, tucking the lower left-hand corner under. Roll it in a diagonal fashion, beginning at the lower right-hand corner, to form the neck. If you find that the neck is rather slender, use an extra bath towel here, to give added thickness and a sturdier shape.

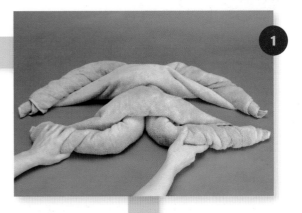

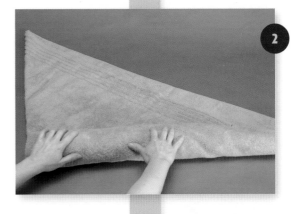

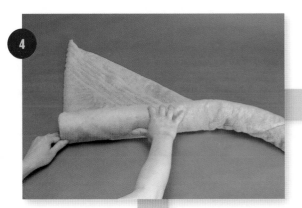

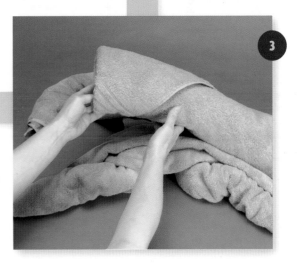

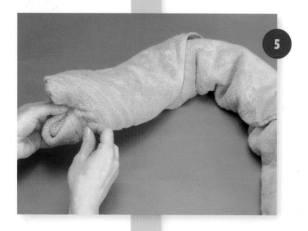

5 Grasp one end of the neck roll and tuck the sides inward to form a pointed mouth. Secure the shape in the center with a small safety pin.

6 Tuck the free end of the neck roll under the body shape and secure it with a large safety pin. Arrange the folds to form a smooth, pleasing line so that the joint between the towel shapes is largely obscured. Now this is the tricky part! You may have to use a few unobtrusive bathroom "props" to raise the neck and hold it in a soft, curved shape. Try to angle the head slightly so that your model takes on a bit of character.

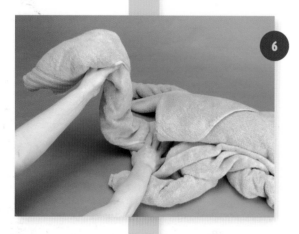

7 Trace onto paper and then cut out the tongue template *(see page 77)*. Cut out the shape from the yellow sponge, and insert the tongue into the mouth.

8 To complete the model, use tabs of double-sided adhesive tape to secure the buttons or eyes in place.

TIP This is quite a long model, so make sure before you begin that you have room to display him to full advantage.

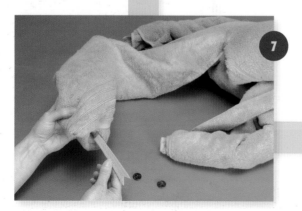

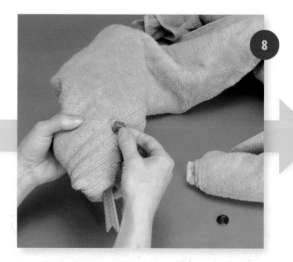

PLESIOSAUR

The Plesiosaur was one of the fiercest hunters in the sea around 150 million years ago—a ferocious beast some 23 ft/7 m in length. People have claimed that "Nessie," the celebrated Loch Ness Monster in Scotland, might be the last surviving Plesiosaur, and this design is based on the famous looping body that has been sighted on the mysterious loch. Leave it afloat on the bed in your spare bedroom and ask your guests to photograph any sightings!

YOU WILL NEED

- 1 green bath towel
- 2 green hand towels
- 2 buttons/plastic eyes
- fixing kit (see page 8)

Make your own Plesiosaur

1 To make the head, lay the green bath towel out vertically, then fold the upper and lower edges to meet at the center. Indicate a crease line in the pile of the towel with your fingertip about 6 in/15 cm in from the right-hand edge. Now fold along the crease line.

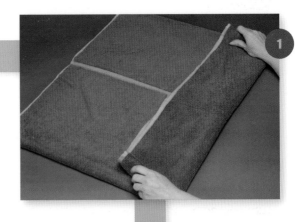

2 Fold the upper and lower corners of the left-hand side inward to meet at the center. Pat the diagonal folds flat using the palm of your hand.

3 Grasp one diagonal fold and roll it toward the center. Do the same with the other fold, to form a long, pointed shape. This will become the head and neck. In order to keep the rolls in place, you need to secure them with a few safety pins.

4 Stand the shape up on the wide end and splay the fold's lower edge out a little, so that it balances steadily. Carefully bend the pointed shape to create the curved head and neck of the mysterious monster.

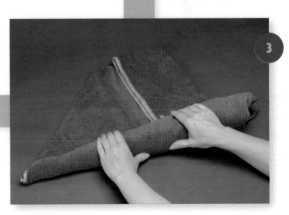

5 To make one of the dinosaur's humps, lay a hand towel out vertically and fold the upper and lower edges to meet at the center. Now make a 4 in/ 10 cm fold along each of the side edges, then pat the folds flat using the palm of your hand.

6 Grasp the lower edge of the folded band and roll it up to form a cylinder. Use a few safety pins to secure the overlap to ensure that the shape does not unroll. Make one more hump in the same way.

7 Bend the rolls gently to form inverted U-shapes. Splay out the folds at each end so that the shapes will stand up steadily by themselves.

8 Place the curved humps in a row behind your Plesiosaur's head. Add two buttons or eyes to the head to complete your very own model of the Loch Ness Monster, then set it afloat the bedcovers.

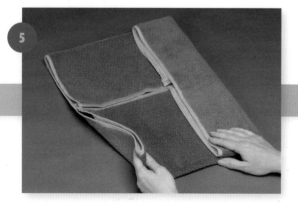

EASY

STONEHENGE

The reason why the prehistoric English monument of Stonehenge was erected has been the subject of much speculation: astronomy, sun worship, human sacrifice? It has been suggested that it may have taken three million hours of megalithic labor to construct such a stone spectacle. But this Stonehenge project will take you about 10 minutes, so you don't need to worry. Try making a simple model of two uprights and one lintel first; then, if you feel particularly creative, why not extend it to the full circular version—depending, of course, on the size of your bathroom!

YOU WILL NEED

- 3 gray bath towels
- fixing kit *(see page 8)*

Make your own Stonehenge

1 Lay one bath towel out horizontally, then fold both short sides to meet at the center point, overlapping the edges slightly. Pat the folds flat using the palm of your hand.

2 Pick up the lower edge of the folded shape and make another fold about 4 in/10 cm deep. Again, smooth out any wrinkles and pat the folds flat using the palm of your hand.

3 Now pick up the fold that runs along the lower edge of the folded shape and make another fold about 4 in/10 cm deep. This forms the lower part of the vertical column. This edge needs to be a little thicker than the top part so that the column will stand up steadily when it is complete.

4 Pick up the upper edge and fold it downward to meet the fold made in step 3.

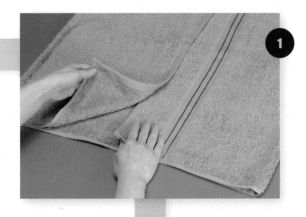

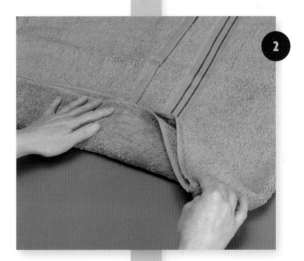

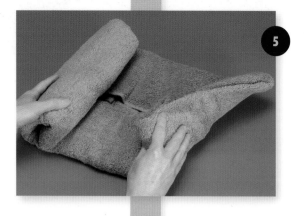

5 Take up the right-hand and left-hand sides in turn and fold each inward to meet at the center point—do not overlap the edges here.

6 Fold the right-hand and left-hand edges to meet at the center again, forming a squat shape, then use safety pins to hold the edges together. Make another column in the same way using the second bath towel, repeating steps 1–6.

7 To make the lintel, lay the remaining bath towel out horizontally. Fold it into three widthways, then roll it up loosely from the lower short end. Use two or three safety pins to secure the overlap, then flip the shape over so that the overlap is on the underside.

8 Stand both vertical columns upright. Open out the folds at the lower edges if they do not stand steadily by themselves. Then place the horizontal slab across the top of the two vertical columns to complete your model.

 MODERATE

EUPLOCEPHALUS

This ferocious, reptile-like creature was part of the plant-eating Ankylosaurus family that roamed mainly in the earth's northern hemisphere. He had few or no teeth in his mouth (after all, it doesn't take much to eat a leaf), but made up for it with an impressive display of spines, spikes, and bony plates on his back, which he used in self-defense. Archaeologists have likened the Euplocephalus to an armor-plated mobile tank.

YOU WILL NEED

- 2 yellow bath towels
- 1 blue bath towel
- 2 buttons/plastic eyes
- 16 colored plastic clothespins
- fixing kit (see page 8)

Make your own Euplocephalus

1 Lay one yellow bath towel out horizontally, then roll it up loosely in a diagonal fashion, beginning at the lower right-hand corner. The resulting roll will be used to wrap the basic body shape and give it extra bulk and height, and to form the head and neck.

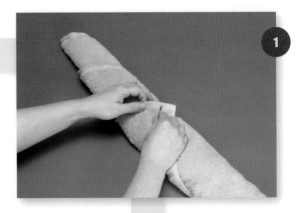

2 Using the second yellow bath towel, construct Body shape 1 *(see page 10)*. Then place it on the center of the roll created in step 1. Wrap the right-hand end of the roll around the body shape, tucking the end under the dinosaur's chest.

3 Lay the blue bath towel out horizontally, then construct Body shape 2b *(see page 11)*. This pointed roll forms the back and tail.

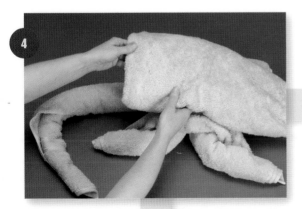

4 Lay the back/tail roll onto the body and legs, with the pointed end to the right. Arrange the folds along the sides of the body above the legs, to make a neat line. You will need to use safety pins to secure the roll, if necessary.

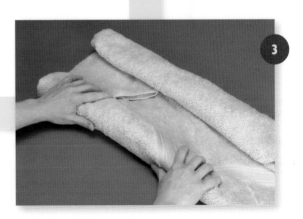

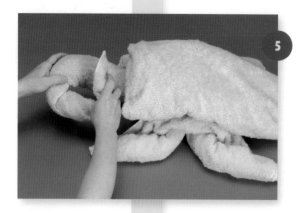

5 With one hand, grasp the roll that you created in step 1 close to the front legs of the dinosaur; then grasp the free end of the roll with your other hand and wind it around itself to form a large knot.

6 Tuck the corner of the roll through the knot and pull it tightly to create a neat, rounded head shape. You may need to coax this shape a little to achieve the desired effect.

7 When you are satisfied with the head shape, use a large safety pin to secure the back of the neck to the body. At this point try to introduce a slight curve to the neck; this will add a little character to your finished model.

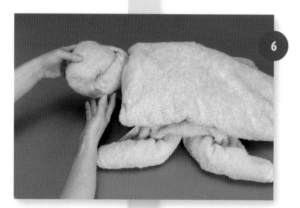

8 To complete the model, use tabs of double-sided adhesive tape to secure the buttons or eyes in place. Then fix the colored plastic clothespins along the back of the Euplocephalus to resemble spines.

TIP If you don't have brightly colored pins to use for the spines, ordinary wooden clothespins will work just as well.

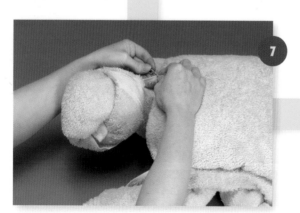

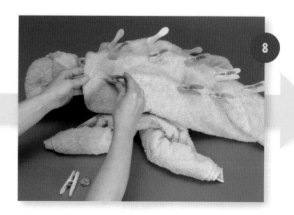

 MODERATE

PTERANODON

For all bedtime bird-spotters, the ultimate in Jurassic towel origami must be the soaring Pteranodon. These magnificent beasts would put a golden eagle to shame, with a wingspan of 30 ft/9 m and long, toothless beaks that were used to catch fish. Pteranodon fossils, found mainly in the chalk beds of Kansas, give us a detailed model on which to base a toweling version that will illuminate the beds of any state.

YOU WILL NEED

- 2 gray bath towels
- 1 gray hand towel
- 2 buttons/plastic eyes
- fixing kit (see page 8)

Make your own Pteranodon

1 Lay one bath towel out horizontally. Make a vertical crease in the pile with your fingertip down the center of the towel, then fold the bottom two corners inward to meet at the center. This shape will form the wings.

2 Gather the towel at the center and draw the fabric together using both hands to form a small bump. Secure the shape with an elastic band. This will be useful to support the head and enable the dinosaur to "fly."

3 Now take the other bath towel and lay it out vertically. Roll the upper and lower short edges to meet at the center. Then flip the shape over to the other side.

4 Grasp the rolled-up shape at both ends and bend it in half, as shown. Now locate the corners of the towel inside each roll, grasp the corners tightly, and pull them outward.

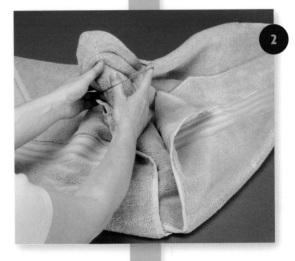

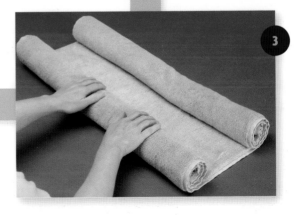

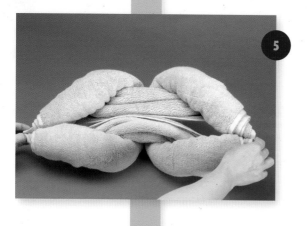

5 You will see that the towel has formed a body shape with four limbs (like Body shape 1 on page 10). Arrange the limbs neatly and secure the center edges with a few safety pins so that the shape does not come undone.

6 To make the head, lay the hand towel out vertically. Bring the lower short edge up to meet the top, then bring both edges down to meet the lower fold. Press all the towel folds flat with the palm of your hand.

7 Beginning at the lower right-hand corner, roll the towel tightly in a diagonal fashion toward the center. Do the same on the other side, to form the pointed head shape that is characteristic of the Pteranodon. Use safety pins to secure the rolls and to position the head on the body shape.

8 Attach the body to the wings created in steps 1 and 2, using safety pins. Secure two buttons or wibbly-wobbly eyes to the head with small tabs of double-sided adhesive tape (or use cut-out felt or card circles as a substitute). You can lay your Pteranodon flat on a bed or, if you're feeling adventurous, suspend him from the shower rail (by tying a string to the elastic band used in step 2).

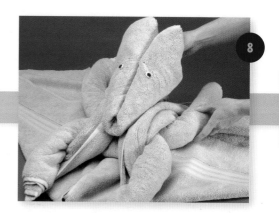

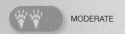
STEGOSAURUS

Now this is what you could call a classic dinosaur! The name means "roof lizard," and although his body is quite large (Steggie can grow up to 25 ft/7.5 m long), he had a small head and a brain the size of a walnut. This chap spent most of his time chewing leaves and wandering around very slowly. He did, however, have a strong tail, which he used to fend off predators. The scaly plates or fins on his back are thought to have been used to regulate his temperature—quite handy in steamy bathroom environments.

YOU WILL NEED

- 3 green bath towels
- 1 green hand towel
- 5 green scouring pads
- 9 wooden clothespins
- 2 buttons/plastic eyes
- fixing kit *(see page 8)*

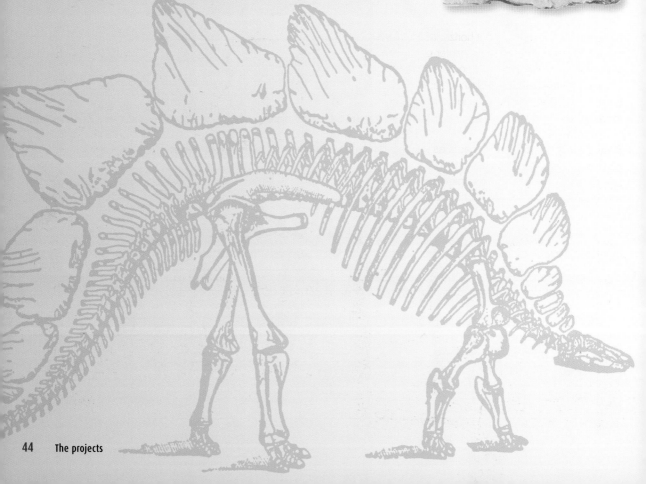

Make your own Stegosaurus

1 Lay one bath towel out horizontally, then roll it up loosely in a diagonal fashion, beginning at the lower right-hand corner. Using a second bath towel, construct Body shape 1 *(see page 10)*. Lay this body shape in the center of the roll just created.

2 Wrap the roll around the body shape, tucking the ends underneath the body, then secure the overlap with a safety pin. The ends of the roll will act as a prop to raise the body shape slightly (you can add extra height by placing some small bars of soap here).

3 Lay the third bath towel out horizontally and fold the left-hand edge to meet the center point. Fold the upper and lower left-hand corners in, forming a point. Roll the bath towel up in a diagonal fashion, beginning at the lower right-hand corner. This roll forms the back and tail.

4 Lay the roll onto the body shape, as shown. You can now arrange the folds along the sides of the body above the legs to make a pleasing line. Then manipulate the tail to form a soft, pointed curve.

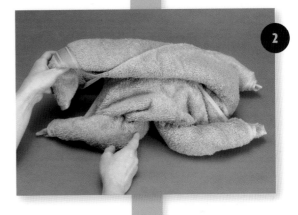

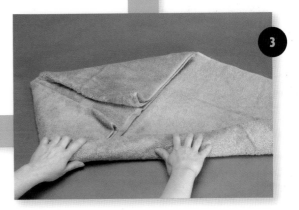

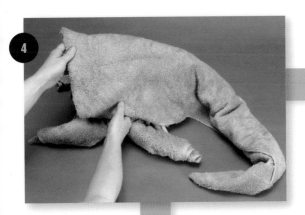

5 To make the head and neck, lay the hand towel out horizontally, then fold both sides to meet at the center. Fold the lower left-hand corner up to meet the center, then roll the towel in a diagonal fashion, beginning at the lower right-hand corner. Use a large safety pin to secure the resulting roll at the center.

6 Tuck the pointed right-hand end of the head and neck roll underneath the body, as shown, securing the roll to the chest with a safety pin. Now fix the back of the neck to the back/tail roll using another safety pin.

7 Trace onto paper and then cut out the fin templates *(see page 78)*. Cut out each fin from the scouring pads, the number of times indicated on each template. Fix the pairs of fins to the clothespins, as shown, with strips of double-sided adhesive tape.

8 To finish the model, secure the fins in size order along the spine of the Stegosaurus, as shown. Then use tabs of double-sided adhesive tape to fix the buttons or eyes in place on the head.

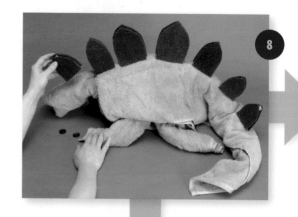

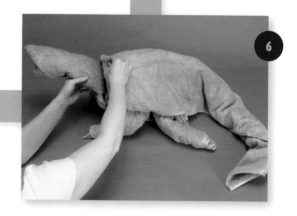

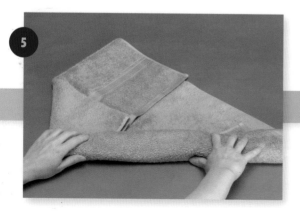

TRICERATOPS

The name literally means "three-horned face," and this dino
had two horns on his brow and another on the tip of his nose.
Triceratops was a herbivore and herd animal, roaming the land
en masse in search of tasty plants to munch. However, when you
have T. rex *(see page 72)* as your neighbor, you have to develop
quite sophisticated means of self-preservation. Triceratops made
good use of his horns in battle, together with the protective
shieldlike neck frill that stood up like a fan from behind his
head when required—quite an impressive sight!

YOU WILL NEED

- 2 yellow bath towels
- 3 yellow face cloths
- 1 yellow hand towel
- 1 yellow kitchen sponge
- 2 buttons/plastic eyes
- fixing kit *(see page 8)*

Make your own Triceratops

1 Lay one bath towel out horizontally, then form Body shape 2a *(see page 11)*. Manipulate the resulting soft, arched shape so that it stands steadily by itself. Open out the ends of the rolls, if necessary, to form a secure base.

2 Lay the other bath towel out horizontally, then fold it in half by bringing the left-hand short edge over to meet the right-hand edge. Roll the shape diagonally from the lower left-hand corner to create a loose, pointed triangular shape. This will form the back and tail.

3 Place the rolled shape on top of the arched legs, as shown, then arrange the right-hand pointed end to form the tail. Tuck the other end down between the rolls at the front, securing it with a few large safety pins. Make sure that the roll is firmly fixed, because it will support the head and neck ruff.

4 To make the neck ruff, fold each face cloth diagonally in half to form a triangle. Grasp the center and gather it together to form a three-pointed shape, securing it on the underside with a safety pin.

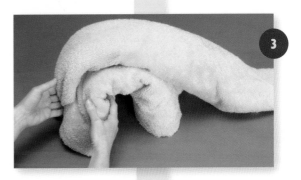

TIP If the legs are too slim, use another bath towel laid on top of the first in step 1, to add thickness. The bulkier leg shape will be more able to stand alone and support the back and tail roll.

5 Lay the hand towel out horizontally. Fold it into thirds and follow Head shape 2 *(see page 14)*, flipping the head shape over and pulling out the points found inside the rolls at the top of the head to form small ears. Secure the rolled shape with two large safety pins and set aside.

6 Place the ruffs from step 4 around the neck, then secure them to the body with safety pins and/or clothespins. Arrange the folds so that they stick out nicely (the clothespins can be used to support the points, or you could tuck tiny soaps into the folds to facilitate this effect).

7 Place the head from step 5 onto the body in front of the ruffs, tucking the pointed ends of the ruffs under the head. Secure the head in place with a few large safety pins (you may need to support the head under the chin using a bottle or toilet roll).

8 Trace onto paper and then cut out the horn template *(see page 77)*. Cut out three horn shapes from the kitchen sponge, then position the horns at the top of the head and on the nose. Secure the horns with dressmaker's pins, then use tabs of double-sided adhesive tape to fix the buttons or eyes in place to complete the model.

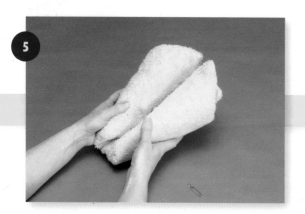

VELOCIRAPTOR

A contemporary of the Tyrannosaurus *(see page 72)*, the Velociraptor was a much smaller, racy-looking dinosaur: agile and quick on its feet, but still sporting a fine set of teeth and powerful jaws. Some of the earliest examples of Velociraptor remains were found in Mongolia's Gobi Desert in the 1920s— and more recently in bathrooms across the nation!

YOU WILL NEED

- 2 red bath towels
- 2 orange hand towels
- 1 plastic milk container or stiff white card
- 2 buttons/plastic eyes
- fixing kit *(see page 8)*

Make your own Velociraptor

1 Lay one bath towel out horizontally. Roll both short ends in toward the center, then proceed to construct Body shape 1 *(see page 10)*. Secure the center folds with a large safety pin.

2 Flip the shape over to the other side, then fix the folds that lie across the center using two large safety pins. This prevents the body shape from working loose as you manipulate the rest of the body. You can now arrange the four "limbs" neatly.

3 Lay the second bath towel out horizontally, then fold it in half by bringing the left-hand short edge over to meet the right-hand edge. Roll up the resulting square diagonally, beginning at the lower right-hand corner, to form a long pointed shape.

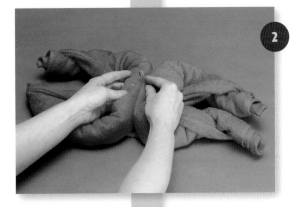

4 Lay the body shape from steps 1 and 2 onto the roll. Pick up the left-hand point of the roll and bring it over the center of the body, then tuck the end under the body shape. Take the right-hand point and bring it up and over the body so that the point overlaps the body on the left-hand side. Secure the overlap with a safety pin.

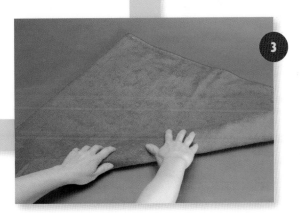

5 Lay one orange hand towel out horizontally, then fold it in half by bringing the left-hand short edge over to meet the right-hand edge. Fold the lower left-hand corner toward the center. Then roll the shape diagonally, beginning at the lower right-hand corner, to form a long roll that is pointed at the right-hand end and blunt at the left.

6 Prop up the body using a shampoo bottle or other container. Now place the roll formed in step 5 onto the body, as shown. Secure it to the back of the body shape with a few large safety pins.

7 Roll up the second orange hand towel in the same way *(see step 5)*, to form the Velociraptor's head and neck. Tuck the pointed end of this roll under the body, then lift up the head/neck and fix the back to the blunt end of the roll that is secured to the body shape. Bend the neck and head to form a pleasing shape.

8 Trace onto paper and then cut out the teeth template *(see page 76)*. Cut out the teeth from a plastic milk container or some stiff white card, as described on page 74. To complete the model, use tabs of double-sided adhesive tape to secure the teeth and the buttons or eyes in place.

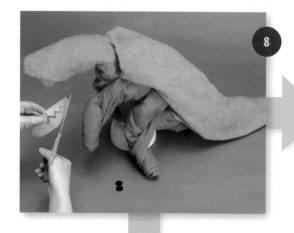

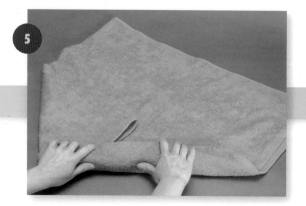

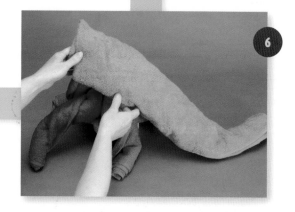

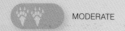

WOOLLY MAMMOTH

The woolly mammoth was similar in appearance to modern African or Indian elephants, but—due to the adverse weather conditions at the time of the last Ice Age—had to grow a lot of hair to keep him from freezing to death. The giant North American mammoth holds the record for being the tallest, at nearly 13 ft/4 m at the shoulder. Our mammoth is slightly more modest in stature and would fit neatly on any bathroom shelf.

YOU WILL NEED

- 2 brown bath towels
- 1 extra bath towel for body padding (any color)
- 1 brown hand towel
- 2 white face cloths
- 2 buttons/plastic eyes
- fixing kit (see page 8)

Make your own woolly mammoth

1 Place one brown bath towel plus the extra bath towel together, then lay them out horizontally. Follow the instructions for Body shape 2a *(see page 11)*, to form a softly curved arch shape that will become the legs.

2 To make the head, lay the second brown bath towel out vertically. Fold the top and lower left-hand corners toward the center, forming an arrowhead shape. Now roll the diagonal folds toward the center in a diagonal fashion, and secure the rolls with a safety pin.

3 Flip the head shape over to the other side and turn down the horizontal edge that lies across the rolls; as you do this, you will see the ears beginning to form. At this point you can arrange the ear flaps into a pleasing shape.

4 Now lay the brown hand towel out horizontally. Follow the instructions for Head shape 2, steps 1 and 2 *(see page 14)*. Secure the rolls with a safety pin.

5 This pointed shape will form the lower jaw and neck, and will act as a support for the main head shape and the tusks. Tuck the end of the jaw/neck in between the front two leg rolls and secure it with a safety pin.

6 Lay one face cloth out in a diamond shape. Fold in the left-hand corner, then roll up the face cloth, beginning at the corner nearest you. Use a few small safety pins to secure the overlap. Repeat with the other face cloth. These form the tusks.

7 Bend each tusk into a shallow curved shape. Now place the top end of each tusk onto the lower jaw, tucking the corner down in between the rolls of the jaw. Secure each tusk in place with a safety pin.

8 Place the head from step 3 onto the body and secure it using a few large safety pins. To complete the model, use tabs of double-sided adhesive tape to fix the buttons or eyes in place.

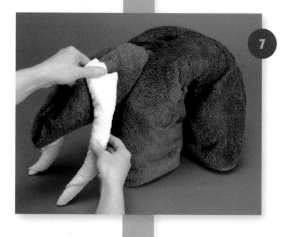

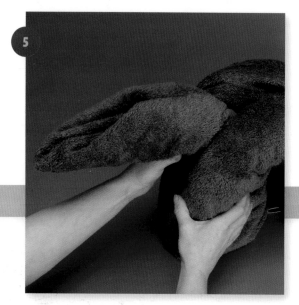

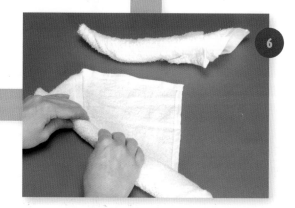

CAVEMAN

Our caveman had to resort to living in a cave in order to keep out of the cold during the last Ice Age—brrrr ... it must have been mighty chilly in those days! You can have lots of fun dressing up your caveman in various items found around the house; we gave ours a spear, but you could arm him with a back-scrubbing brush or even a loofah!

YOU WILL NEED

- 2 peach bath towels
- 1 extra bath towel for body padding (any color)
- 1 peach hand towel
- 1 pair of peach rubber gloves
- 2 beige elastic hairbands
- 1 pair of black rubber gloves
- 1 striped hand towel
- 2 plastic eyes
- wooden stick for a spear (optional)
- fixing kit (see page 8)

Make your own caveman

1 Lay one peach bath towel out vertically. Fold and roll the extra bath towel, following the instructions for Body shape 3, step 1 *(see page 12)*, then place it in the center of the peach towel close to the top edge. Continue to form Body shape 3 as shown in steps 2–4 *(see page 12)*.

2 Secure the overlap with safety pins. Grasp the shape and sit it on a toilet roll or other container to give the body support and raise it slightly. Arrange the legs neatly on each side to give added stability and obscure the support.

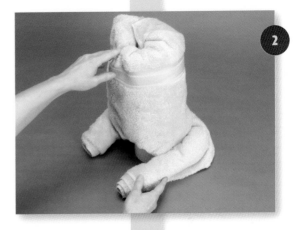

3 To make the caveman's arms, lay the peach hand towel out horizontally and roll it up, beginning at the lower long edge. Place the roll over the top of the body shape and secure it with safety pins. Tuck each end of the roll into a peach-colored rubber glove to form his hands.

4 Lay the second peach bath towel out horizontally, then fold it in half by bringing the left-hand short edge over to meet the right-hand edge. Then follow steps 1 and 2 of Head shape 3 *(see page 14)*.

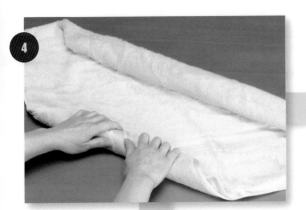

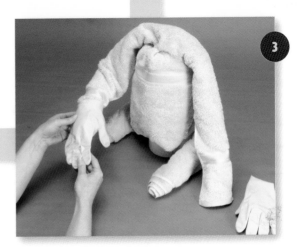

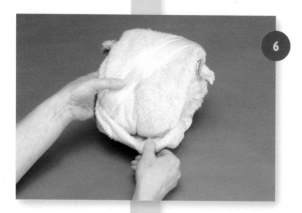

5 Now follow the instructions for steps 3 and 4 on page 14, rolling up the head shape from the closed end, then grasping the outer layer of the open end and peeling it right back over the rolled ball to form the mouth. Secure the overlap with a safety pin.

6 Take the head and pull out a little towel fabric from each side near the top. Wind beige hairbands tightly around the fabric to form two small rounded ears. You can now shape the mouth.

7 Place the caveman's head onto his shoulders and secure two black rubber gloves to the back of the head with clothespins. Arrange the fingers over the top of his head to resemble hair.

8 Make the striped hand towel into a tiger-striped robe to respect caveman's modesty. To complete the model, use tabs of double-sided adhesive tape to secure the plastic eyes in place. Just for fun, give him a spear so that he looks primitive and savage!

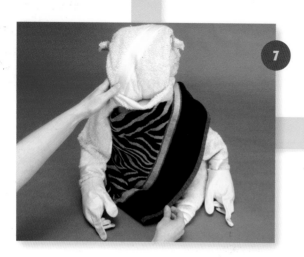

DIMORPHODON

The Dimorphodon was thought to have been the oldest
pterosaur, or flying reptile, residing in the Jurassic period, but
fossilized remains recently have revealed older species dating
from some 15 million years earlier. Dimorphodon is characterized
by his large head, which is often even larger than his body. While
quite at home on the wing, he also liked to run around on land
using his long tail to steady himself. Have fun "flying" this model
from the shower rail to impress your houseguests.

YOU WILL NEED

- 2 blue bath towels
- 1 gray bath towel
- 1 blue hand towel
- 1 blue elastic hairband
- 2 buttons/plastic eyes
- fixing kit (see page 8)

Make your own Dimorphodon

1 Lay one blue bath towel out horizontally, then roll it up in a diagonal fashion, beginning at the lower right-hand corner. This will hold the main body shape together and will also form the tail.

2 To make the wings, lay the gray bath towel out horizontally on top of the body shape. Fold both upper corners toward the center to form a triangular shape, overlapping them slightly. Pick up the bottom point and fold it up toward the center of the triangle. Pat all the folds flat with the palm of your hand.

3 Using the second blue bath towel, construct Body shape 1 (see page 10). With the wings from step 2 on the roll constructed in step 1, place the body shape on top of both, as shown.

4 Grasp the top of the roll formed in step 1 and bring it down in front of the body. Tuck the point under the body at the base. Use several large safety pins to hold all the folds in place—this is very important when you "fly" your model later on.

5 To make the head, lay the blue hand towel out horizontally, then fold it in half by bringing the left-hand short edge over to meet the right-hand edge. Fold the upper and lower left-hand corners to meet the diagonal center of the square. Roll the shape diagonally, starting with the left-hand point, to form the head and neck.

6 Bend the pointed shape almost in half, then wind the blue hairband twice around the shape, about 6 in/15 cm from the folded end, to form a square head shape and the indication of a neck.

7 Lay the head and neck onto the chest created in step 4, and secure the pointed ends to the chest with large safety pins. Now flip the shape over and secure the underside of the head to the shoulders—you don't want Dimorphodon's head to fall off as he flies over the bath!

8 Pin the head and neck to the body and wing structure. To complete the model, use tabs of double-sided adhesive tape to secure the buttons or eyes in place. To display him, use clothespins to suspend the wing tips from your shower rail.

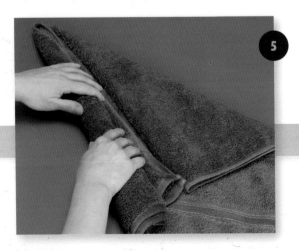

SABER-TOOTHED TIGER

More accurately this carnivore is called the Smilodon, which means "chisel tooth." This powerful Ice Age predator had characteristic bladelike canine teeth, which were used for inflicting fatal wounds on his prey. Although our tiger has indeed got an impressive set of pearly whites, he's really a pussy cat underneath!

YOU WILL NEED

- 4 black and beige striped/patterned bath towels
- 1 extra bath towel for body padding (any color)
- 2 black elastic hairbands
- 1 plastic milk container or stiff white card
- 2 buttons/plastic eyes
- fixing kit (see page 8)

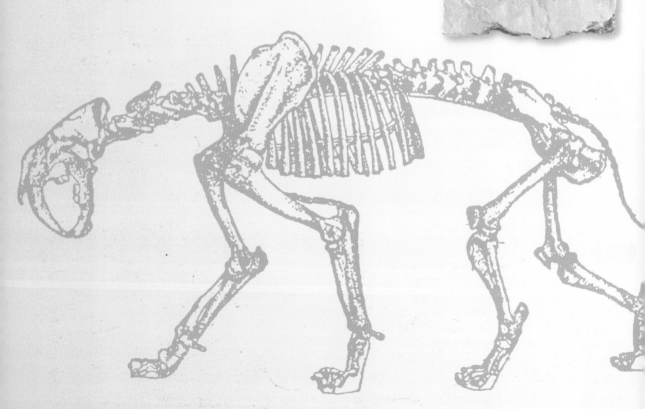

Make your own saber-toothed tiger

1 Lay one striped/patterned bath towel out horizontally. Fold and roll the extra bath towel following the instructions given for Body shape 3, steps 1–4 *(see page 12)*. Pin the overlap securely with large safety pins.

2 Flip the shape over and support the body shape under the "belly," sitting it on a toilet roll or other container to give a little height under the hind legs. Then arrange the legs neatly to disguise the support.

3 Lay another striped/patterned bath towel out horizontally, then roll it up, beginning at the lower edge. Lay out the third striped/patterned bath towel in the same way, but roll it up diagonally, beginning at the lower right-hand corner.

4 Bend the third towel in half to form a softly arched shape, then prop it up against the shoulders of the seated body shape to form the front legs. Secure the shoulders to the body with a few safety pins. The legs will also act as supports. Use the diagonally rolled second towel to form the tiger's tail.

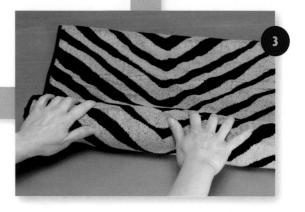

5 Take the last striped/patterned bath towel and form Head shape 1 *(see page 13)*. Wind the two black hairbands tightly around the top two corners of the head to form small rounded ears.

6 For the tiger's saberlike teeth, trace onto paper and then cut out the teeth template *(see page 79)*. Wrap the template around the plastic milk container, trace around it, then remove the template. Cut out the shape carefully, following the traced outline.

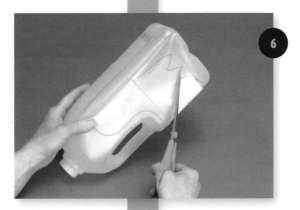

7 Open up the tiger's mouth and insert the saberlike teeth. You may need to use a tab or two of double-sided adhesive tape to make sure that they stay in place.

8 Position the head on the shoulders, using safety pins to secure it in place. To complete the model, use tabs of double-sided adhesive tape to secure the buttons or eyes in position.

TYRANNOSAURUS REX

The name Tyrannosaurus rex means "Tyrant king." This fellow was reputed to be one of the largest and most ferocious carnivorous dinosaurs to roam the earth during the Cretaceous period; he could grow up to 46 ft/14 m long and 20 ft/6 m high. T. rex also sported razor-sharp teeth and claws, a massive head, and powerful jaws. Actually, if our caveman *(see page 60)* had been around at this time, T. rex would probably have been able to swallow him whole. However, we've made our Tyrannosaurus rex a lovely raspberry-pink color—not so scary now, eh?

YOU WILL NEED

- 2 pink bath towels
- 1 extra bath towel for body padding (any color)
- 2 pink elastic hairbands
- 1 pink hand towel
- 1 plastic milk container or stiff white card
- 2 buttons/plastic eyes
- fixing kit *(see page 8)*

Make your own Tyrannosaurus rex

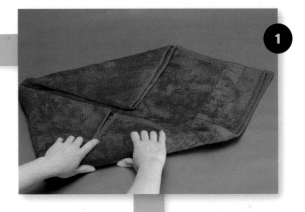

1 Lay one pink bath towel out horizontally, then fold it in half by bringing the left-hand short edge over to meet the right-hand edge. Fold in the upper and lower left-hand and the lower right-hand corners to meet at the center. Now roll both sides to meet at the center, forming a pointed shape *(see Body shape 2b, steps 1–3 on page 11)*.

2 Fold and roll the extra bath towel to form the body padding *(see Body shape 2a, step 1 on page 11)*. Lay the other pink bath towel out vertically, place the rolled-up pad on top, and wrap it to form Body shape 3 *(see steps 2 and 3 on page 12)*. Grasp the short ends of the bath towel at the top and wrap a pink hairband around each corner, as shown, to form two short arms.

3 Grasp the lower short end of the pink bath towel and roll it up toward the base of the padded body. Secure the roll to the body at the center, using a large safety pin, to form the hind legs. Now grasp the body shape and flip it over so that the overlap between the arms and hind legs is on the underside.

4 You will need to support the body shape under the belly and hind legs with a shampoo bottle or toilet roll in a neutral color, because your Tyrannosaurus rex won't be able to stand up by himself!

5 Lay the rolled-up pointed shape from step 1 onto the propped-up body, placing the blunt end at the neck and arranging the pointed tail to act as an extra prop for the body shape. You can secure the rolled shape with a few safety pins, if you wish.

6 To make the head, lay the pink hand towel out horizontally, then roll both short ends toward the center, to about a quarter of the way across the width. You can now begin to construct Head shape 1 *(see page 13)*. This is quite a tricky shape to complete —you may need a few attempts to get it just right!

7 Trace onto paper and then cut out the teeth template *(see page 76)*. Place the paper template around a plastic milk container, trace around the outline with a pencil, then remove the template. Cut carefully along the traced lines with sharp scissors.

8 Insert the plastic teeth into T. rex's mouth—this may require a little clever dentistry, using a tab or two of double-sided tape. Fix the head to the body with a few large safety pins, then secure the buttons or eyes in place with more tabs of double-sided tape.

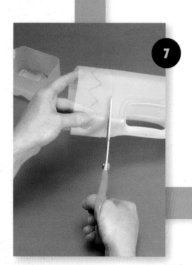

TIP You can make the teeth from a sheet of stiff white card if you don't have a plastic bottle—or even from the back of an old greeting card.

TEMPLATES

Tyrannosaurus rex teeth
Enlarge by 140%
Cut one from plastic milk container/card

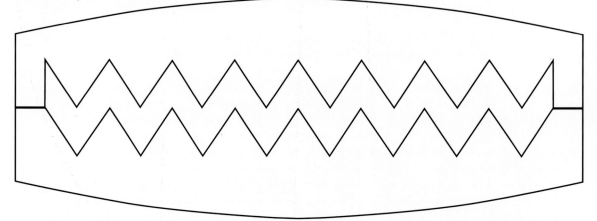

Velociraptor teeth
Cut one from plastic milk container/card

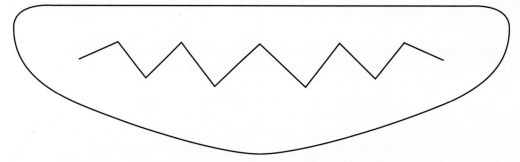

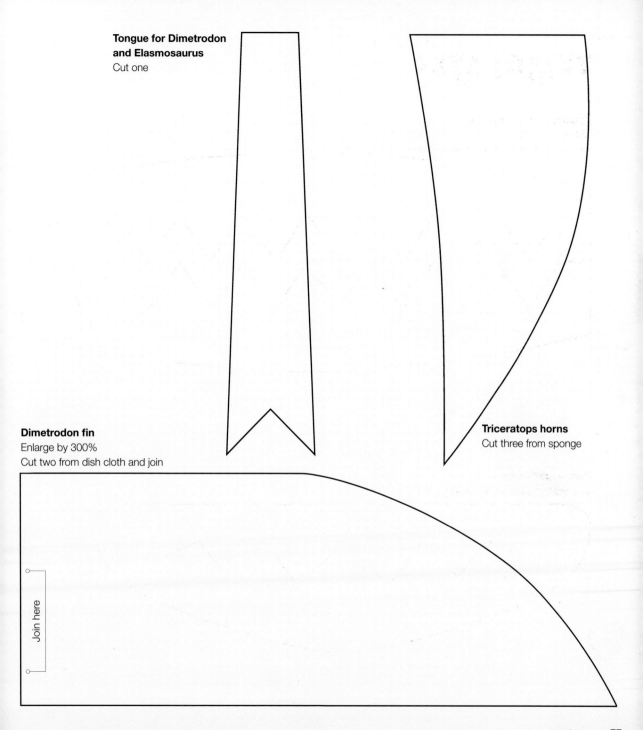

**Tongue for Dimetrodon
and Elasmosaurus**
Cut one

Triceratops horns
Cut three from sponge

Dimetrodon fin
Enlarge by 300%
Cut two from dish cloth and join

Join here

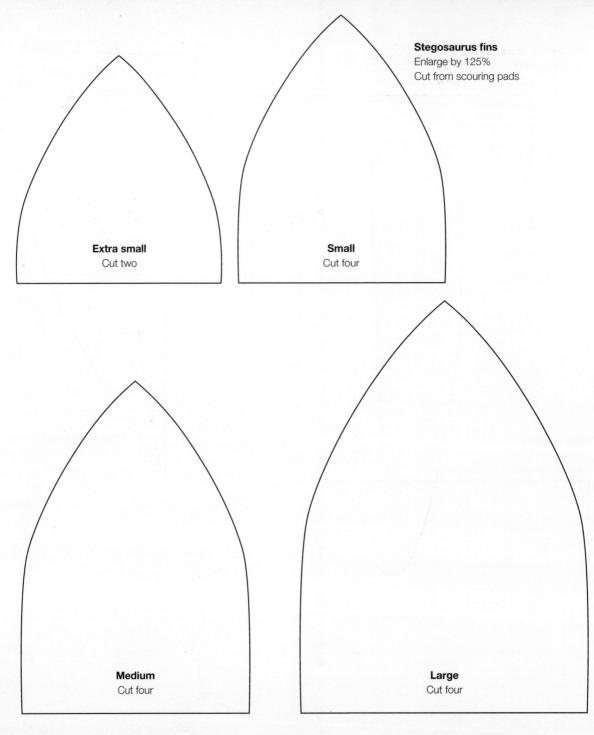

Extra small
Cut two

Small
Cut four

Stegosaurus fins
Enlarge by 125%
Cut from scouring pads

Medium
Cut four

Large
Cut four

Saber-toothed tiger teeth
Enlarge by 160%
Cut one from plastic milk container

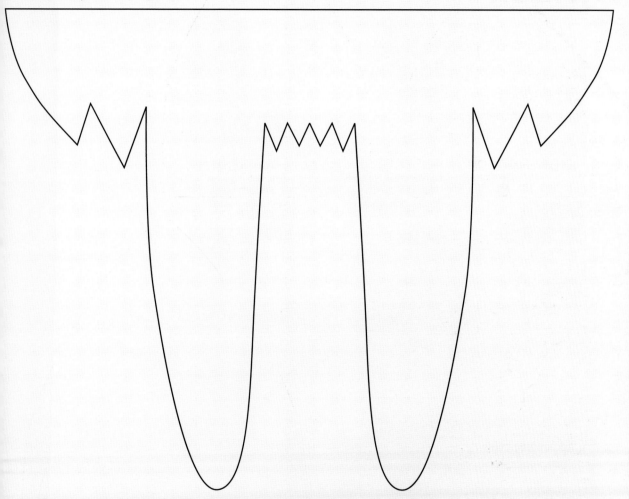

INDEX

Acknowledgments
Christy Towels: www.christy-home.com